PIZZA
AND
ANTIPASTI

BRIMAR

Editor Angela Rahaniotis
Graphic Design Zapp
Photography Marc Bruneau
Food Preparation / Stylist Josée Robitaille
Assistant Stylist Marc Maula

©1994 Brimar Publishing Inc.
338 Saint Antoine St. East
Montreal, Canada H2Y 1A3
Tel. (514) 954-1441
Fax (514) 954-5086

ISBN 2-89433-136-3
Printed in Canada

PIZZA AND ANTIPASTI

Everybody loves pizza! But many
home cooks think pizza is too
complicated to make from scratch.

This cookbook will show you otherwise,
with easy, step-by-step recipes
for pizza dough and an exciting variety
of sauces and toppings that will turn you
into an expert in no time at all.

In addition, this book contains a
wonderful selection of delicious antipasti –
the Italian approach to starters and
snacks. Your family and friends will rave
over these flavour-packed and healthy
salads, dips, marinated vegetables,
and hors d'oeuvres.

And with the full-colour photographs
accompanying each recipe, you will
be able to turn out antipasti and pizzas
that will tantalize the eye as well as
the tastebuds.

Bruschetta
(6 to 10 servings)

50 ml	extra virgin olive oil	2 fl oz
2	large tomatoes, peeled, seeded and chopped	2
30 ml	chopped fresh basil	2 tbsp
3	garlic cloves, peeled, crushed and sliced	3
8	anchovy fillets, drained	8
10	slices French baguette, toasted	10
	salt and pepper	

1 Heat half of olive oil in frying pan over high heat. Add tomatoes and basil; season and cook 4 minutes. Remove pan from heat.

2 Heat remaining oil in small saucepan. Add garlic and anchovy fillets; cook 2 minutes.

3 Place about 15 ml (1 tbsp) of tomato mixture on each slice of bread. Top with garlic and anchovy fillets. Season well and serve.

Hot Chicken Croquettes
(4 to 6 servings)

225 g	cooked chicken, finely diced	8 oz
375 ml	White Sauce, heated (see page 38)	12 fl oz
2	slices cooked ham, minced	2
30 g	grated Parmesan cheese	1 oz
3	eggs	3
5 ml	extra virgin olive oil	1 tsp
150 g	white breadcrumbs	5 oz
	salt and freshly ground pepper	
	few drops of hot pepper sauce	
	pinch of nutmeg	
	oil for deep frying	

1 Place chicken, white sauce, ham, cheese and 1 egg in bowl. Mix together and season well. Add hot pepper sauce and pinch of nutmeg. If preferred, mixture can be prepared in food processor.

2 Refrigerate mixture 15 minutes.

3 Shape chilled mixture into small croquettes. Beat remaining eggs with extra virgin olive oil. Dip croquettes in beaten eggs, then roll in breadcrumbs.

4 Deep fry in hot oil until golden. Serve with spicy sauce.

Broccoli and Cauliflower Insalata
(6 servings)

1	head broccoli, in small florets	1
1	small head cauliflower, in florets	1
1	small courgette, sliced	1
1	sweet red pepper, chopped	1
6	artichoke hearts, marinated in oil	6
70 g	stoned Kalamata olives	2 1/2 oz
6	anchovy fillets, drained and chopped	6
6	garlic cloves, blanched and puréed	6
15 ml	chopped fresh parsley	1 tbsp
15 ml	chopped fresh basil	1 tbsp
75 ml	olive oil	2 1/2 fl oz
60 g	Gorgonzola cheese, crumbled	2 oz
	juice of 1 1/2 lemons	
	salt and pepper	

1 Blanch broccoli in boiling, salted water for 2 minutes. Remove from pan and place immediately under cold, running water. Drain and set aside.

2 Add cauliflower and courgette to boiling water. Blanch 3 minutes. Place vegetables under cold, running water. Drain and set aside.

3 Place broccoli, cauliflower, courgette and chopped red pepper in large bowl. Slice artichoke hearts in half and add to bowl. Toss in olives and mix well.

4 Place anchovies in small bowl. Add garlic, herbs and lemon juice; whisk together. Pour in oil and whisk until incorporated. Season dressing with pepper and pour over salad ingredients.

5 Toss salad, correct seasoning and marinate 20 minutes at room temperature. Sprinkle with cheese before serving.

Blanch broccoli in boiling, salted water for 2 minutes. Remove from pan and place immediately under cold, running water. Drain and set aside.

Add cauliflower and courgette to boiling water. Blanch 3 minutes. Place vegetables under cold, running water. Drain and set aside.

Slice artichoke hearts in half and add to bowl. Toss in olives and mix well.

Place anchovies in small bowl. Add garlic, herbs and lemon juice; whisk together. Pour in oil and whisk until incorporated. Season dressing with pepper and pour over salad ingredients.

Eggs à la Grecque
(4 servings)

3	leeks, white part only	3
24	white button onions, peeled	24
450 g	fresh mushroom caps, cleaned	1 lb
4	garlic cloves, peeled	4
375 ml	dry white wine	12 fl oz
125 ml	water	4 fl oz
30 ml	tomato paste	2 tbsp
2	bay leaves	2
4	fresh basil leaves	4
12	black peppercorns	12
1 ml	thyme	¼ tsp
4	cold poached eggs	4
	juice of ½ lemon	
	salt and pepper	

1 Slit leeks from top to bottom twice, leaving 2.5 cm (1 in) intact at base. Wash leeks under cold, running water to remove grit and sand. Slice thinly.

2 Place leeks in boiling, salted water. Add a few drops of lemon juice and cook 6 minutes over medium heat. Remove leeks and drain well.

3 Transfer leeks to saucepan and add remaining ingredients, except eggs. Cook 15 minutes over low heat.

4 Serve leek mixture over cold poached eggs.

Cauliflower and Hard-Boiled Eggs
(4 to 6 servings)

1	large cauliflower, in florets and blanched	1
8	anchovy fillets, drained and chopped	8
100 g	stoned black olives, sliced	3½ oz
45 ml	capers	3 tbsp
30 ml	chopped fresh basil	2 tbsp
50 ml	balsamic vinegar	2 fl oz
125 ml	extra virgin olive oil	4 fl oz
2	hard-boiled eggs, quartered	2
	salt and pepper	

1 Place blanched cauliflower in bowl. Add anchovies, olives and capers. Season well and add basil; mix carefully.

2 Place vinegar, salt and pepper in separate bowl. Add olive oil and whisk together.

3 Pour vinaigrette over salad and toss lightly. Marinate 15 minutes. Serve garnished with hard-boiled eggs.

Mozzarella au Gratin

(6 to 8 servings)

6	slices Italian bread, 8 mm (1/3 in) thick	6
375 ml	milk	12 fl oz
160 g	grated mozzarella cheese	5 1/2 oz
30 ml	plain flour	2 tbsp
2	large eggs, beaten	2
45 ml	olive oil	3 tbsp
45 g	butter	1 1/2 oz
	salt and pepper	

1 Remove crusts from bread. Dip slices of bread in milk.

2 Divide cheese among 3 slices of bread. Season well and cover with remaining bread to make sandwiches. Cut sandwiches in half.

3 Sprinkle flour over sandwiches, then dip each in beaten eggs.

4 Heat oil and butter in large frying pan over medium heat. Fry sandwiches 2 to 3 minutes on each side or until cheese is melted and sandwiches are browned.

5 Blot sandwiches on absorbent kitchen paper, then cut into small squares. Serve hot.

Stuffed Courgettes
(4 to 6 servings)

3	courgettes	3
3	large sweet yellow peppers	3
50 ml	olive oil	2 fl oz
4	large tomatoes, peeled, seeded and chopped	4
2	garlic cloves, peeled, crushed and chopped	2
45 ml	chopped fresh basil	3 tbsp
12	slices Caciocavallo cheese	12
	salt and pepper	
	few drops of extra virgin olive oil	

Preheat grill to 200°C (400°F, mark 6).

1 Slice courgettes in half lengthways. Using melon baller, scoop out most of courgette flesh, leaving shell intact. Place shells in boiling water for 1 minute. Remove and set aside to drain.

2 Cut yellow peppers in half and remove seeds. Oil skin and place cut-side-down on baking sheet; grill 6 to 8 minutes. Remove and place in large bowl. Cover bowl with cling film. Let peppers steam 3 minutes. Peel and discard skins. Slice peppers thinly.

3 Heat oil in frying pan over medium heat. Add tomatoes, garlic and basil; season well. Bake 10 minutes. Add sliced peppers.

4 Arrange courgette shells in baking dish. Fill with tomato pepper mixture and cover with slices of cheese. Drizzle a few drops of extra virgin olive oil over cheese.

5 Grill 2 minutes, or until cheese melts.

Prawn Cheese Spread
(6 to 10 servings)

45 ml	olive oil	3 tbsp
450 g	fresh prawns, peeled, deveined and quartered	1 lb
3	shallots, peeled and chopped	3
2	garlic cloves, peeled, crushed and chopped	2
1	small chilli pepper, seeded and chopped	1
225 g	full fat soft cheese	½ lb
60 g	pimiento pepper, chopped	2 oz
	salt and pepper	
	few drops of lime juice	

1 Heat oil in frying pan over medium heat. Add prawns, shallots, garlic and chilli pepper; season well. Cook 4 minutes, stirring once.

2 Cool, then transfer mixture to food processor. Blend several seconds and add remaining ingredients. Blend until combined. Correct seasoning.

3 Serve on toasted bread or crackers or as a stuffing for celery sticks.

Anchovy and Garlic Dip
(6 to 10 servings)

1 litre	double cream	1¾ pt
12	anchovy fillets, drained and finely chopped	12
4	garlic cloves, peeled, crushed and finely chopped	4
	salt and freshly ground pepper	
	cayenne pepper to taste	

1 Pour cream into saucepan, season and bring to boil. Cook over low heat until reduced by half.

2 Add anchovies and garlic. Simmer 6 minutes.

3 Pour into fondue dish and keep warm while serving.

Use this dip for fresh vegetables and toasted bread sticks.

Sicilian Ratatouille
(6 to 8 servings)

2	large aubergines, diced	2
125 ml	olive oil	4 fl oz
3	onions, peeled and sliced	3
3	garlic cloves, peeled, crushed and chopped	3
4	large tomatoes, peeled, seeded and chopped	4
45 ml	capers	3 tbsp
75 g	stoned olives	2½ oz
45 ml	white wine vinegar	3 tbsp
15 ml	honey	1 tbsp
	salt and pepper	

1 Spread aubergines in one layer in large container. Sprinkle with salt and let stand 40 minutes at room temperature. Drain well and set aside.

2 Heat half of oil in large frying pan over medium heat. Add onions and cook 18 minutes over low heat. Do not let burn.

3 Add garlic, tomatoes, capers and season well. Continue cooking 10 minutes. Stir in olives.

4 Heat remaining oil in separate large frying pan over medium heat. Add aubergines, season and cook 15 minutes.

5 Add tomato mixture to aubergines. Add vinegar and honey. Mix well and correct seasoning. Continue cooking 16 minutes to evaporate all liquid.

6 Serve cold on small rounds of toasted bread.

Toasted Italian Bread with Marinated Tomatoes
(6 servings)

3	garlic cloves, blanched and puréed	3
45 ml	extra virgin olive oil	3 tbsp
2	large tomatoes, peeled, seeded and roughly chopped	2
30 ml	chopped fresh basil	2 tbsp
6	thick slices Italian bread	6
6	slices Fontina cheese	6
8	anchovy fillets, drained and chopped	8
	salt and freshly ground pepper	

Preheat oven to 180°C (350°F, mark 4).

1 Place garlic in mixing bowl. Add olive oil and whisk together to incorporate. Add tomatoes and basil; mix well. Season and marinate 30 minutes at room temperature.

2 Arrange slices of Italian bread on baking sheet. Divide cheese among slices and top with chopped anchovies. Season with pepper.

3 Bake 6 minutes in oven or until cheese melts.

4 Using slotted spoon, top each portion with marinated tomato mixture. Season with freshly ground pepper and serve.

Celeriac Remoulade
(4 to 6 servings)

1	large celeriac, peeled and grated	1
1	large egg yolk	1
15 ml	French mustard	1 tbsp
3	garlic cloves, blanched and puréed	3
15 ml	lemon juice	1 tbsp
125 ml	olive oil	4 fl oz
15 ml	chopped fresh parsley	1 tbsp
	juice of 1 lemon	
	salt and pepper	
	lettuce leaves	

1 Cook grated celeriac in boiling, salted, acidulated water for 5 minutes. Place under cold, running water to stop cooking process. Drain and squeeze out excess liquid.

2 Place celeriac in large bowl with juice of 1 lemon. Mix, cover and set aside.

3 Place egg yolk, mustard, garlic and 15 ml (1 tbsp) lemon juice in small bowl. Season with salt and pepper. Whisk ingredients together.

4 Add oil in thin stream while whisking constantly. If mixture becomes too thick, add more lemon juice. Pour over celeriac; mix well. Add parsley, season and serve on lettuce leaves.

Pesto on Baguette
(6 to 8 servings)

30 g	fresh basil, washed and dried	1 oz
20 g	fresh curly parsley, washed and dried	¾ oz
20 g	fresh Italian parsley, washed and dried	¾ oz
5	garlic cloves, peeled	5
75 g	grated Parmesan cheese	2½ oz
35 g	pine nuts	1¼ oz
125 ml	olive oil	4 fl oz
75 ml	mayonnaise	3 fl oz
2	French baguettes	2
	few drops of lime juice	
	salt and freshly ground black pepper	
	cayenne pepper to taste	
	grated mozzarella cheese (optional)	

1 Place basil, all parsley and garlic in food processor. Blend several seconds. Add Parmesan cheese and pine nuts; blend again to incorporate.

2 Add oil through hole in top while blending. Mixture should be thoroughly blended. Transfer to bowl and stir in mayonnaise and lime juice. Season well with salt, black pepper and cayenne pepper.

3 Cut baguettes in half lengthways and grill until lightly toasted. Remove and let cool.

4 Spread pesto over baguettes and grill 1 minute. If desired, top bread with grated mozzarella cheese and grill 1 more minute. Slice and serve warm.

Braised Whole Leeks
(serves 4 to 6)

900 g	leeks, white part only	2 lb
250 ml	dry white wine	8 fl oz
250 ml	water	8 fl oz
125 ml	olive oil	4 fl oz
3	garlic cloves, peeled	3
12	peppercorns	12
1	bay leaf	1
1	sprig fresh thyme	1
6	fresh basil leaves	6
	juice of 2 lemons	
	salt and pepper	

1 Slit leeks from top to bottom twice, leaving 2.5 cm (1 in) intact at base. Wash leeks under cold, running water to remove grit and sand.

2 Place leeks and all ingredients in frying pan over medium heat. Bring to boil.

3 Cook 35 minutes over low heat. When cooked, remove from heat and let leeks cool in marinade.

4 Serve leeks with some of the marinade.

Spicy Scallops
(4 servings)

30 ml	olive oil	2 tbsp
350 g	fresh scallops, cleaned and sliced	¾ lb
30 ml	chopped fresh basil	2 tbsp
2	garlic cloves, peeled, crushed and chopped	2
1	jalapeño pepper, seeded and chopped	1
225 g	fresh mushrooms, cleaned and halved	½ lb
24	seedless cucumber balls	24
45 ml	balsamic vinegar	3 tbsp
135 ml	extra virgin olive oil	4½ fl oz
	salt and pepper	
	lettuce leaves	

1 Heat oil in frying pan over medium heat. Add scallops and increase heat to high. Cook 1 minute on each side. Add basil, garlic and jalapeño pepper and season well. Cook 1 more minute.

2 Remove scallops from pan and set aside in bowl. Add mushrooms to hot pan and cook 3 minutes over high heat. Add more oil if needed.

3 Add mushrooms to scallops in bowl. Mix in cucumber.

4 Mix vinegar with extra virgin olive oil; season well. Pour over salad, toss to incorporate and serve on lettuce leaves.

Braised Fennel in Olive Oil
(4 to 6 servings)

3	large fennel bulbs	3
125 ml	olive oil	4 fl oz
3	garlic cloves, peeled	3
1	sprig fresh thyme	1
12	fresh basil leaves	12
12	peppercorns	12
2	bay leaves	2
1	chilli pepper, seeded and sliced	1
	juice of 1 lemon	
	salt and pepper	
	water	
	lemon wedges	
	chopped fresh basil	
	lettuce leaves	

1 Remove stems and green leaves from fennel bulbs. Peel bulbs and cut in half. Slice into strips lengthways.

2 Place fennel in frying pan. Add all ingredients, except lemon, chopped basil and lettuce leaves, with just enough water to cover. Season and bring to boil.

3 Cook 30 minutes over low heat or until tender. Do not cover. If liquid evaporates too quickly, replenish as needed.

4 Let cool in marinade. Serve on lettuce leaves with some of the marinade. Garnish with fresh lemon wedges and chopped basil, if desired.

Prosciutto with Stuffed Figs
(4 servings)

8	fresh figs, cut in half	8
15 ml	crystallised mixed fruit	1 tbsp
15 ml	honey	1 tbsp
40 g	chopped mixed nuts	1½ oz
225-350 g	prosciutto	½-¾ lb
	lemon slices	

1 Scoop out 5 ml (1 tsp) of flesh from each fig half. Place flesh in bowl and add crystallised fruit and honey; mix well. Add mixed nuts and mix again. Stuff figs.

2 Arrange slices of prosciutto decoratively on serving platter. Position stuffed figs and garnish with lemon slices.

Tuna and White Beans
(4 to 6 servings)

2	tins (540 ml/19 oz each) white beans, drained	2
50 ml	olive oil	2 fl oz
15 ml	lemon juice	1 tbsp
3	spring onions, chopped	3
2	garlic cloves, peeled, crushed and chopped	2
30 ml	chopped fresh Italian parsley	2 tbsp
15 ml	chopped fresh basil	1 tbsp
1	tin (184 g/6.5 oz) tuna, packed in oil, well drained	1
	salt and pepper	
	lettuce leaves	

1 Place beans in mixing bowl.

2 Pour oil into small bowl and add lemon juice; season well. Add spring onions and garlic. Mix well. Add parsley and basil; mix again.

3 Pour vinaigrette over beans and mix well. Flake tuna and add to bowl. Mix, correct seasoning and serve salad on lettuce leaves.

Cooked Marinated Mushroom Caps
(4 to 6 servings)

50 ml	dry white wine	2 fl oz
125 ml	olive oil	4 fl oz
30 ml	water	2 tbsp
2	bay leaves	2
4	garlic cloves	4
12	peppercorns	12
6	fresh basil leaves	6
1	sprig fresh thyme	1
450 g	small fresh mushroom caps, cleaned	1 lb
	juice of 1 lemon	
	salt and freshly ground black pepper	
	cayenne pepper to taste	

1 Place all ingredients, except mushrooms, in saucepan. Bring to boil and cook 10 minutes over medium heat.

2 Add mushrooms to saucepan, season and mix. Cook 6 to 8 minutes over low heat.

3 Let mushrooms cool in marinade. Serve.

Salad of Mussels and Artichoke Hearts
(4 servings)

1.4 kg	fresh mussels, cleaned and bearded	3 lb
125 ml	dry white wine	4 fl oz
1	shallot, peeled and chopped	1
15 ml	chopped fresh parsley	1 tbsp
15	artichoke hearts, marinated in oil	15
4	fresh basil leaves	4
75 g	stoned black olives	2 1/2 oz
90 g	feta cheese, diced	3 oz
45 ml	wine vinegar	3 tbsp
125 ml	olive oil	4 fl oz
1 ml	oregano	1/4 tsp
	salt and pepper	
	lettuce leaves	

1 Place mussels in saucepan with wine, shallot and parsley. Cover and cook 4 minutes over medium heat or until shells open. Discard any unopened shells.

2 Remove mussels from shells and place in mixing bowl. Drain artichokes and cut in quarters; add to bowl. Mix in basil leaves, olives and feta cheese. Season well.

3 Place vinegar, oregano, salt, and pepper in separate bowl. Add oil and whisk together. Pour over mussels and mix well. Correct seasoning and serve on lettuce leaves.

Artichokes, Italian Style
(4 to 6 servings)

12	very small fresh artichokes	12
250 ml	dry white wine	8 fl oz
125 ml	olive oil	4 fl oz
125 ml	water	4 fl oz
12	peppercorns	12
12	small shallots, peeled	12
1	bay leaf	1
2	garlic cloves, peeled	2
	juice of 1½ lemons	
	salt and pepper	

1 Place all ingredients in saucepan. Bring to boil.

2 Cook artichokes 45 minutes over low heat. If liquid evaporates too quickly, replenish with combination of wine and water.

3 When artichokes are cooked, remove from heat and let cool in marinade.

4 Serve artichokes with some of marinade. Do not strain.

5 Accompany with fresh tomato sauce, if desired.

Aubergine Croustade
(6 to 8 servings)

50 ml	olive oil	2 fl oz
1	onion, peeled and chopped	1
3	garlic cloves, peeled, crushed and chopped	3
1	small aubergine, diced	1
3	tomatoes, peeled, seeded and chopped	3
1 ml	crushed chillies	¼ tsp
30 ml	chopped fresh basil	2 tbsp
12	slices Italian bread, toasted	12
12	anchovy fillets, drained	12
12	slices Scamorze cheese	12
	freshly ground pepper	
	few drops of extra virgin olive oil	

1 Heat oil in frying pan over medium heat. Add onion and garlic; cook 4 minutes over low heat.

2 Add aubergine, tomatoes and seasonings. Cook 20 minutes over medium heat.

3 Let mixture cool to room temperature, then spread over toasted bread. Top with anchovy fillets and cheese. Drizzle a few drops of extra virgin olive oil over cheese. Season generously with pepper. Grill 3 minutes and serve.

Tomatoes with Bocconcini
(4 servings)

2	bunches fresh basil	2
4	medium tomatoes	4
24	large cubes of Bocconcini cheese	24
50 ml	balsamic vinegar	2 fl oz
125 ml	olive oil	4 fl oz
	salt and freshly ground pepper	

1 Remove stems from fresh basil. Wash leaves and dry well.

2 Core tomatoes and cut in wedges. Place in mixing bowl with cheese and remaining ingredients, including fresh basil. Mix and marinate 30 minutes at room temperature.

3 Spoon tomatoes, cheese and basil on serving platter. Pour juices from bowl over ingredients. Serve.

White Bean and Prawn Mélange
(4 to 6 servings)

45 ml	olive oil	3 tbsp
1	red onion, peeled and sliced in rings	1
½	celery stick, sliced	½
2	garlic cloves, peeled and minced	2
450 g	fresh prawns, peeled and deveined	1 lb
1 ml	crushed chillies	¼ tsp
60 g	pimiento pepper, chopped	2 oz
275 g	cooked white beans	10 oz
45 ml	lemon juice	3 tbsp
90 ml	extra virgin olive oil	3 fl oz
30 ml	chopped fresh basil	2 tbsp
	salt and pepper	

1 Heat 45 ml (3 tbsp) olive oil in frying pan over medium heat. Add onion, celery and garlic; season well. Cook 6 minutes over low heat.

2 Add prawns and crushed chillies. Increase heat to high and cook 3 to 4 minutes, stirring occasionally.

3 Transfer mixture to bowl. Add pimiento and white beans; season well. Mix in lemon juice and extra virgin olive oil. Add basil, mix and marinate 15 minutes at room temperature.

Balsamic Marinated Mushrooms
(4 to 6 servings)

450 g	fresh mushrooms, cleaned and thinly sliced	1 lb
3	spring onions, chopped	3
45 ml	balsamic vinegar	3 tbsp
125 ml	olive oil	4 fl oz
15 ml	chopped fresh basil	1 tbsp
	juice of 2 lemons	
	salt and pepper	

1 Place mushrooms in mixing bowl. Add lemon juice, mixing to moisten all mushrooms. Add spring onions.

2 Mix vinegar, oil, salt and pepper together in small bowl. Pour over mushrooms and mix well. Add basil and mix again.

3 Cover and marinate 1 hour in refrigerator. Serve mushrooms with some of the marinade.

Salad of Potatoes, Beans and Seafood
(4 to 6 servings)

3	potatoes, boiled unpeeled	3
125 g	cooked white beans	¼ lb
75 g	stoned black olives, sliced	2½ oz
90 ml	extra virgin olive oil	3 fl oz
2	garlic cloves, peeled, crushed and chopped	2
10 ml	chopped fresh parsley	2 tsp
10 ml	chopped fresh basil	2 tsp
3	anchovy fillets, drained and chopped	3
30 ml	capers	2 tbsp
225 g	fresh prawns, cooked, shelled and deveined	½ lb
90 g	cooked crabmeat	3 oz
	juice of 1 or 2 lemons	
	salt and black pepper	
	cayenne pepper to taste	

1 Peel potatoes and cut in half. Place in bowl with beans and olives. Set aside.

2 Heat olive oil in frying pan over medium heat. Add garlic, parsley, basil and anchovies. Cook 1 minute. Add capers and lemon juice to taste; season well. Cook 30 seconds.

3 Stir and pour hot mixture over salad ingredients. Mix well and correct seasoning. Add cayenne pepper to taste.

4 Add prawns and crabmeat. Mix and marinate 30 minutes at room temperature before serving.

Grilled Peppers and Tomatoes
(4 to 6 servings)

6	sweet peppers	6
50 ml	extra virgin olive oil	2 fl oz
4	tomatoes, cored and sliced	4
2	garlic cloves, peeled and thinly sliced	2
8	anchovy fillets, drained and chopped	8
8	fresh basil leaves	8
	salt and pepper	

1 Cut peppers in half and remove seeds. Oil skin and place cut-side-down on baking sheet; grill 10 minutes. Remove and let cool. Peel and discard skins. Slice peppers thinly.

2 Arrange sliced grilled peppers on serving platter; drizzle with some of the olive oil. Cover with sliced tomatoes.

3 Add garlic and anchovy fillets; season well. Drizzle with remaining oil and top with basil leaves. Marinate 18 minutes at room temperature before serving.

Fresh Mussels with Dolcelatte Cheese
(4 to 6 servings)

900 g	fresh mussels, scrubbed and bearded	2 lb
50 ml	dry white wine	2 fl oz
400 g	cooked white beans	14 oz
2	shallots, peeled and chopped	2
2	garlic cloves, peeled, crushed and chopped	2
30 ml	chopped fresh basil	2 tbsp
15 ml	capers	1 tbsp
15 ml	Italian mustard	1 tbsp
50 ml	extra virgin olive oil	2 fl oz
90 g	Dolcelatte cheese, crumbled	3 oz
	salt and freshly ground pepper	
	lemon juice	

1 Place mussels in saucepan with wine. Cover and cook 5 to 6 minutes over medium heat, or until shells open.

2 Discard any unopened shells. Remove mussels from shells and transfer to bowl. Add white beans, shallots, garlic, basil and capers; season well.

3 Mix mustard, olive oil and lemon juice to taste together in separate bowl. Pour mixture over mussels and mix well.

4 Add cheese, mix and let marinate 15 minutes before serving.

Grilled Yellow Pepper Antipasto
(4 to 6 servings)

6	sweet yellow peppers	6
90 g	Fontina cheese, cut in julienne	3 oz
75 g	stoned green olives	2½ oz
50 ml	extra virgin olive oil	2 fl oz
15 ml	French mustard	1 tbsp
30 ml	double cream	2 tbsp
	salt and freshly ground pepper	
	lettuce leaves	

1 Cut peppers in half and remove seeds. Oil skin and place cut-side-down on baking sheet; grill 6 to 8 minutes. Remove and place in large bowl. Cover bowl with cling film. Let peppers steam 3 minutes. Peel and discard skins. Slice peppers thinly.

2 Place peppers in bowl with all remaining ingredients. Mix well and correct seasoning.

3 Marinate 30 minutes at room temperature. Serve on lettuce leaves.

How to Peel and Seed Fresh Tomatoes

1 Core fresh tomatoes.

2 Place briefly in pot with boiling water, just long enough to loosen skins.

3 Remove tomatoes from pot and set aside to cool slightly. When cool enough to handle, peel off skins.

4 Slice tomatoes in half, horizontally. Grasp tomato half in hand, with cut side facing down. Squeeze out seeds into bowl.

5 Chop or dice tomatoes.

Basic Fresh Tomato Sauce

5	tomatoes, cored	5
30 ml	olive oil	2 tbsp
1	onion, peeled and chopped	1
3	garlic cloves, peeled, crushed and chopped	3
250 ml	dry white wine	8 fl oz
45 ml	chopped fresh basil	3 tbsp
1	small chilli pepper, seeded and chopped	1
	salt and pepper	

1 Plunge tomatoes into saucepan with boiling water. Remove tomatoes after 1 minute. When cool enough to handle, remove skins. Cut tomatoes in half, horizontally and squeeze out seeds. Chop pulp and set aside.

2 Heat oil in frying pan over medium heat. Add onion and garlic; cook 4 minutes.

3 Increase heat to high and pour in wine; cook 3 minutes.

4 Add remaining ingredients, including reserved tomato pulp, and bring to boil. Reduce heat to low and cook sauce 30 minutes. Do not cover. Stir occasionally.

5 Let sauce cool before refrigerating. Sauce can be stored, covered, up to 3 days.

Fresh Tomato Sauté

50 ml	olive oil	2 fl oz
3	shallots, peeled and chopped	3
3	garlic cloves, peeled, crushed and chopped	3
250 ml	dry white wine	8 fl oz
5	tomatoes, cored, peeled and seeded	5
15 ml	basil	1 tbsp
5 ml	oregano	1 tsp
1 ml	crushed chillies	¼ tsp
45 ml	chopped sun-dried tomatoes	3 tbsp
	salt and pepper	

1 Heat oil in frying pan over medium heat. Add shallots and garlic; cook 3 minutes over low heat.

2 Add wine, increase heat to high, and cook 2 minutes.

3 Chop tomatoes and add to pan. Add seasonings and sun-dried tomatoes. Bake 10 minutes over high heat.

4 Reduce heat to low. Continue cooking mixture 5 to 8 minutes.

5 Cool before refrigerating. Sauce can be stored, covered, up to 3 days.

Pesto Sauce

8	garlic cloves	8
60 g	fresh basil leaves, washed and dried	2 oz
60 g	grated Parmesan cheese	2 oz
125 ml	olive oil	4 fl oz
	salt and pepper	

1 Place unpeeled garlic cloves in saucepan with 250 ml (8 fl oz) water. Bring to boil and cook 4 minutes. Remove cloves from water and let cool. Peel cloves and place in food processor.

2 Add basil and cheese to garlic. Season well and blend several minutes until puréed.

3 While machine is blending, pour oil in thin stream through hole in top. Ingredients should be well blended.

4 To store pesto, transfer mixture to glass jar. Place piece of cling film on surface of pesto and press down with fingers. Seal jar with tight-fitting lid. Sauce can be stored in refrigerator up to 3 days.

White Sauce

60 g	butter	2 oz
½	onion, chopped	½
60 ml	plain flour	4 tbsp
500 ml	milk, heated	¾ pt
	salt and white pepper	
	pinch of nutmeg	

1 Heat butter in saucepan over medium heat. Add onion and cook 2 minutes over low heat.

2 Stir in flour and continue cooking 1 minute.

3 Pour in milk, whisking constantly. Season well and add nutmeg. Cook sauce 8 to 10 minutes over low heat. Stir 3 to 4 times during cooking process.

4 Pass sauce through sieve into clean bowl. Cover with sheet of greaseproof paper, touching surface of sauce, and let cool before refrigerating.

5 This sauce will keep 2 to 3 days in refrigerator, covered.

Spicy Gazpacho Sauce

1	celery stick, diced	1
1	tomato, peeled, seeded and quartered	1
1	sweet green pepper, diced	1
1	jalapeño pepper, seeded and chopped	1
2	shallots, peeled and chopped	2
2	garlic cloves, peeled	2
2 ml	oregano	½ tsp
250 ml	chicken stock, heated	8 fl oz
15 ml	cornflour	1 tbsp
45 ml	cold water	3 tbsp
	salt and pepper	

1 Place celery, tomato, green pepper, jalapeño pepper, shallots, garlic and oregano in food processor. Blend well.

2 Transfer mixture to saucepan. Pour in chicken stock and season well. Cook sauce 10 minutes over medium heat.

3 Dilute cornflour in cold water. Stir into sauce and cook 1 minute over low heat to thicken. Transfer sauce to bowl and let cool before refrigerating.

4 Sauce can be stored in refrigerator, covered, up to 3 days.

Rouille Pizza Spread

4	sweet red peppers	4
7	garlic cloves, unpeeled	7
30 ml	white breadcrumbs	2 tbsp
125 ml	olive oil	4 fl oz
	salt and pepper	

1 Cut red peppers in half and remove seeds. Oil skin and place cut-side-down on baking sheet; grill 6 minutes. Remove and let cool. Peel off skin and set aside.

2 Place unpeeled garlic cloves in saucepan with 250 ml (8 fl oz) water. Bring to boil and cook 4 minutes. Remove cloves from water and let cool. Peel cloves and place in food processor.

3 Add red peppers to food processor and blend with garlic until puréed. Add breadcrumbs and season well; blend again.

4 While machine is blending, pour oil in thin stream through hole in top. Ingredients should be well combined. Depending on consistency, add more oil if desired, up to 50 ml (2 fl oz).

5 Correct seasoning, cover and keep refrigerated up to 3 days, until ready to use.

Ratatouille Sauce

1	sweet yellow pepper	1
1	sweet red pepper	1
30 ml	olive oil	2 tbsp
1	onion, peeled and chopped	1
3	garlic cloves, peeled, crushed and chopped	3
2	shallots, peeled and chopped	2
1	medium aubergine with skin, diced	1
1	small courgette, diced	1
4	tomatoes, peeled, seeded and chopped	4
30 ml	chopped fresh basil	2 tbsp
1 ml	thyme	¼ tsp
	salt and pepper	

1 Cut peppers in half and remove seeds. Oil skin and place cut-side-down on baking sheet; grill 6 minutes. Remove and let cool. Peel off skin, slice thinly and set aside.

2 Heat oil in frying pan over medium heat. Add onion, garlic and shallots; cook 4 minutes.

3 Add aubergine, season well and continue cooking 6 minutes. Add courgette and cook 3 minutes.

4 Add remaining ingredients, mix well and cook 30 minutes over low heat. Stir occasionally.

5 Keep covered in refrigerator for up to 3 days, until ready to use.

Thick Pizza Sauce

60 ml	olive oil	4 tbsp
1	onion, peeled and chopped	1
3	garlic cloves, peeled, crushed and chopped	3
2	tins (796 ml/28 oz each) plum tomatoes	2
1	tin (156 ml/5½ oz) tomato purée	1
30 ml	chopped fresh basil	2 tbsp
15 ml	chopped fresh oregano	1 tbsp
1	chilli pepper, seeded and chopped	1
2 ml	thyme	½ tsp
1	bay leaf	1
	salt and pepper	
	pinch of sugar	

1 Heat oil in large frying pan over medium heat. Add onion and garlic; cook 3 minutes over low heat.

2 Chop tomatoes and add to pan with juice. Stir in tomato purée and remaining ingredients. Mix well.

3 Cook sauce, uncovered, 1 hour over low heat. Stir occasionally. Sauce should become thick. Refrigerate for up to 3 days, covered, until ready to use.

Tips on Making Pizza

●

Always bake pizza in a very hot oven and on the lower oven rack.
The simplest way is to use a solid or perforated pizza pan.

●

For a crisp crust, grease pizza pan with olive oil.

●

Supermarkets have a good selection of ready-made pizza dough
shells and ready-to-use pizza dough.

●

When making your own dough, be sure the water temperature
is correct and that you have a warm place for the dough to rise.

●

Rolling out pizza dough to just the right thickness takes some
practice. Rotate dough frequently and turn dough over during rolling to
maintain round shape. The final thickness of the dough is a matter
of taste. The thinner the crust, the crispier the pizza will be.

●

You may roll out pizza dough in different shapes other
than circular: square, rectangular, triangular, etc.

●

Always crimp edges of pizza dough shell to prevent sauce from
spilling over. Spread sauce over pizza dough shell but not completely
to edges. Leave about a 2.5-cm (1-in) border.

●

The recipes give measurements for sauce and cheese. Depending
on your preference and the type of pizza dough shell used, you may
choose to decrease or increase the quantities suggested.

Basic Pizza Dough
two 36-cm (14-in) pizzas

300 ml	lukewarm water*	½ pt
15 ml	dried yeast	1 tbsp
440 g	plain flour	15 oz
5 ml	salt	1 tsp
50 ml	olive oil	2 fl oz
	pinch of sugar	

*It is important that water temperature be very close to 43 °C (110 °F).

1 Place 50 ml (2 fl oz) lukewarm water in mixing bowl. Sprinkle yeast over water and let stand 2 minutes. Add pinch of sugar and cover bowl. Set aside in warm place for 5 to 6 minutes, until yeast starts to foam.

2 Place flour and salt in large mixing bowl. Make a well in centre and pour in yeast. Add remaining water and oil; mix dough with fingers.

3 Once dough is well mixed, gather into ball and place on floured work surface. Knead dough 10 minutes until smooth and elastic.

4 Shape into ball and place in oiled bowl. Cover with cling film and let rise 2 hours in warm place.

5 Cut dough in half. Roll out each piece on floured work surface until desired thickness is reached. Rotate dough during rolling process to produce a round shape of even thickness.

6 Crimp edges of crust. Garnish pizza and bake.

Vegetarian Pizza
36-cm (14-in) pizza

6	slices yellow summer squash	6
6	slices courgette	6
5	slices red onion rings	5
1/2	sweet green pepper, sliced	1/2
1/2	sweet yellow pepper, sliced	1/2
4	slices Italian aubergine*	4
45 ml	olive oil	3 tbsp
175 ml	Thick Pizza Sauce (see p. 42)	6 fl oz
1	pizza dough shell	1
100 g	grated mozzarella cheese	3 1/2 oz
6	cherry tomatoes, halved	6
1	garlic clove, peeled and sliced	1
	salt and freshly ground pepper	

Preheat oven to 260°C (500°F, mark 10).

1 Change oven setting to grill. Baste all vegetables, except cherry tomatoes, with oil. Place in roasting tin and grill 4 minutes. Season vegetables and set aside.

2 Reset oven to original temperature.

3 Spread pizza sauce over pizza dough shell. Add grilled vegetables and cheese.

4 Arrange cherry tomatoes and sprinkle with garlic. Season well with pepper.

5 Bake 10 to 12 minutes in oven.

*Italian aubergine, often called baby aubergine, is much smaller than the regular variety and has a more delicate skin.

Courgette Pizza
36-cm (14-in) pizza

45 ml	olive oil	3 tbsp
1	onion, peeled and chopped	1
2	garlic cloves, peeled, crushed and chopped	2
1	jalapeño pepper, seeded and chopped	1
1	courgette, sliced 5 mm (¼ in) thick	1
30 ml	chopped fresh basil	2 tbsp
250 ml	Ratatouille Sauce (see p. 41)	8 fl oz
1	pizza dough shell	1
135 g	grated mozzarella cheese	4½ oz
	pinch of thyme	
	salt and freshly ground pepper	

Preheat oven to 260°C (500°F, mark 10).

1 Heat oil in frying pan over medium heat. Add onion and cook 4 minutes. Add garlic, jalapeño pepper and courgette. Add all seasonings, mix and cook 6 minutes over high heat.

2 Spread ratatouille sauce over pizza dough shell. Cover pizza with courgette mixture and top with cheese. Season with pepper.

3 Bake 10 to 12 minutes in oven.

Focaccia Bread
(6 to 8 servings)

250 ml	lukewarm water	8 fl oz
2 ml	sugar	½ tsp
15 ml	dried yeast	1 tbsp
300 g	unbleached white flour	11 oz
30 g	butter	1 oz
½	onion, finely chopped	½
15 g	chopped fresh basil	½ oz
60 ml	olive oil	4 tbsp
	salt	

1 Place water, sugar and yeast in mixing bowl. Set aside in warm place for 10 minutes.

2 Add ¾ of flour to yeast and mix well. Set aside to rise in warm place for 2½ hours.

3 Heat butter in frying pan over medium heat. Add onion and cook 10 minutes over low heat. Add basil and continue cooking 2 minutes. Set aside.

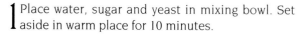

4 Add remaining flour, pinch of salt and half of oil to dough. Mix well and add water if needed. Turn out onto floured work surface and knead 10 minutes.

5 Place dough in oiled bowl. Cover with cling film and let rise another 2 hours in warm place.

6 Using a rolling pin, shape dough into rectangular shape, about 30 x 40 cm (12 x 16 in). Slide onto baking sheet and top with onion and basil garnish. Drizzle with remaining olive oil. Bake 14 to 18 minutes in oven preheated at 230°C (450°F, mark 8). Serve warm.

Quattro Pizza Pie
36-cm (14-in) pizza

4	slices prosciutto	4
60 ml	olive oil	4 tbsp
12	fresh mushrooms, cleaned and sliced	12
175 ml	Thick Pizza Sauce (see p. 42)	6 fl oz
1	pizza dough shell	1
8	slices mozzarella cheese	8
12	stoned black olives, sliced	12
4	artichoke hearts, marinated in oil, drained and quartered	4
	freshly ground pepper	

Preheat oven to 260°C (500°F, mark 10).

1 Slice prosciutto into strips 1 cm (½ in) wide; set aside.

2 Heat 45 ml (3 tbsp) oil in frying pan over medium heat. Add mushrooms, season and cook 3 minutes. Set aside.

3 Spread pizza sauce over pizza dough shell. Cover with slices of mozzarella cheese.

4 Arrange olives, artichoke hearts, prosciutto and mushrooms separately on pizza, each ingredient covering ¼ of pizza pie.

5 Season with pepper and drizzle remaining oil over ingredients.

6 Bake 10 to 12 minutes in oven.

Pizza with Prosciutto, Tomato and Cheese
36-cm (14-in) pizza

175 ml	Basic Fresh Tomato Sauce (see p. 35)	6 fl oz
1	pizza dough shell	1
90 g	prosciutto, sliced in strips	3 oz
100 g	mozzarella cheese, diced	3½ oz
6	fresh basil leaves	6
2	garlic cloves, peeled and thinly sliced	2
30 ml	grated Parmesan cheese	2 tbsp
	freshly ground pepper	
	few drops of olive oil	

Preheat oven to 260°C (500°F, mark 10).

1 Spread tomato sauce over pizza dough shell. Add prosciutto, mozzarella cheese and basil leaves.

2 Sprinkle garlic, then Parmesan over pizza. Season generously with pepper and sprinkle with a few drops of olive oil.

3 Bake 10 to 12 minutes in oven.

Super Stuffed Minced Beef Pizza
46-cm (18-in) pizza

45 ml	olive oil	3 tbsp
2	onions, peeled and sliced	2
2	garlic cloves, peeled, crushed and chopped	2
1	sweet yellow pepper, sliced	1
3	anchovy fillets, drained and chopped	3
225 g	lean minced beef	½ lb
1	pizza dough shell*	1
150 g	Caciocavallo cheese, diced	⅓ lb
	pinch of crushed chillies	
	salt and pepper	

Preheat oven to 230 °C (450 °F, mark 8).

1 Heat 30 ml (2 tbsp) oil in frying pan over medium heat. Add onions, garlic and yellow pepper. Season and cook 8 minutes.

2 Add anchovies and minced beef; season and continue cooking 4 minutes. Stir in crushed chillies.

3 Brush *46-cm (18-in) pizza dough shell with oil. Spread filling on one half of dough. Add cheese and fold other side of dough over filling. Crimp edges shut.

4 Place dough on oiled baking sheet. Brush exposed side of dough with oil. Bake 20 minutes in oven.

Pizza Stuffed with Spinach and Cheese
46-cm (18-in) pizza

700 g	fresh spinach, washed and trimmed	1½ lb
45 g	butter	1½ oz
2	garlic cloves, peeled, crushed and chopped	2
60 g	chopped anchovies	2 oz
125 g	ricotta cheese	¼ lb
15 ml	olive oil	1 tbsp
1	pizza dough shell*	1
90 g	grated Gruyère cheese	3 oz
	salt and pepper	

Preheat oven to 230°C (450°F, mark 8).

1 Steam spinach for 3 minutes. Drain well and chop.

2 Heat butter in frying pan over medium heat. Add spinach and garlic; cook 3 minutes.

3 Transfer mixture to bowl. Add anchovies and ricotta cheese; mix well. Season with salt and pepper.

4 Brush oil over *46-cm (18-in) pizza dough shell. Spread spinach filling on ½ of dough. Top with Gruyère cheese and season with pepper. Fold other side of dough over filling. Crimp edges shut.

5 Place dough on oiled baking sheet. Brush exposed side of dough with oil. Bake 20 minutes in oven.

Pecorino Pizza with Pesto
36-cm (14-in) pizza

125 ml	Pesto Sauce (see p. 37)	4 fl oz
1	pizza dough shell	1
100 g	grated mozzarella cheese	3½ oz
2	large tomatoes, cored	2
2	garlic cloves, peeled and sliced	2
1	chilli pepper, seeded and finely chopped	1
4	fresh basil leaves	4
50 g	grated Pecorino cheese	1½ oz
	salt and pepper	

Preheat oven to 260 °C (500 °F, mark 10).

1 Spread pesto sauce over pizza dough shell. Cover with grated mozzarella cheese.

2 Slice tomatoes about 1 cm (½ in) thick and arrange on pizza. Season well and add garlic, chilli pepper and basil leaves.

3 Top with Pecorino cheese.

4 Bake 10 to 12 minutes in oven.

Tex-Mex Pizza Pie
36-cm (14-in) pizza

2	sweet yellow peppers	2
75 g	grated mozzarella cheese	2½ oz
1	pizza dough shell	1
2	tomatoes, sliced 8 mm (⅓ in) thick	2
1	jalapeño pepper, seeded and finely chopped	1
1	garlic clove, peeled, crushed and finely chopped	1
15 ml	chopped fresh basil	1 tbsp
50 g	grated Pecorino Sardo cheese	2 oz
	freshly ground pepper	

Preheat oven to 260°C (500°F, mark 10).

1 Cut yellow peppers in half and remove seeds. Oil skin and place cut-side-down on baking sheet; grill 6 minutes. Remove and let cool. Peel off skin, slice thinly and set aside.

2 Sprinkle mozzarella cheese over pizza dough shell. Arrange tomato slices on cheese.

3 Add yellow peppers and jalapeño pepper. Add garlic and basil. Top with Pecorino Sardo cheese and season well with pepper.

4 Bake 10 to 12 minutes in oven.

Pesto and Prawn Pizza
36-cm (14-in) pizza

45 ml	olive oil	3 tbsp
1/2	courgette, sliced	1/2
225 g	prawns, peeled and deveined	1/2 lb
6	artichoke hearts, marinated in oil, drained and halved	6
125 ml	Pesto Sauce (see p. 37)	4 fl oz
1	pizza dough shell	1
1	tomato, sliced	1
135 g	grated mozzarella cheese	4 1/2 oz
	salt and freshly ground pepper	

Preheat oven to 260 °C (500 °F, mark 10).

1 Heat oil in frying pan over medium heat. Add courgette and cook 2 minutes over high heat.

2 Add prawns and artichoke hearts; season well. Continue cooking 2 minutes over high heat; set aside.

3 Spread pesto sauce over pizza dough shell. Arrange tomato slices and cover with cheese.

4 Bake 10 to 12 minutes in oven.

5 About 2 minutes before pizza is done, top with prawn and vegetable mixture and season well with pepper. Complete baking.

Sweet Pepper Pizza with Caciocavallo Cheese
36-cm (14-in) pizza

3	sweet red peppers	3
2	sweet yellow peppers	2
I	sweet banana pepper	I
60 ml	olive oil	4 tbsp
3	garlic cloves, peeled, crushed and chopped	3
I	chilli pepper, seeded and finely chopped	I
30 ml	chopped fresh basil	2 tbsp
I	bay leaf	I
I	pizza dough shell	I
225 g	diced Caciocavallo cheese	½ lb
	freshly ground pepper	
	few drops of extra virgin olive oil	

1 Cut red and yellow peppers and banana pepper in half and remove seeds. Oil skin and place cut-side-down on baking sheet; grill 18 minutes. Turn peppers over once during cooking. Remove and place in large bowl. Cover bowl with cling film. Let peppers steam 3 minutes. Peel and discard skins. Slice peppers.

2 Transfer sliced peppers to clean bowl. Add oil, garlic, chilli pepper, basil and bay leaf. Season with pepper. Marinate 2 hours. Remove bay leaf.

3 Preheat oven to 260 °C (500 °F, mark 10).

4 Brush extra virgin olive oil over pizza dough shell. Add cheese and top with marinated peppers.

5 Bake 10 to 12 minutes in oven.

Meat, Onion and Red Pepper Pizza
36-cm (14-in) pizza

45 ml	olive oil	3 tbsp
1/2	red onion, chopped	1/2
2	garlic cloves, peeled, crushed and chopped	2
1/2	sweet red pepper, thinly sliced	1/2
3	Italian sausages, meat removed from casings	3
175 ml	Thick Pizza Sauce (see p. 42)	6 fl oz
1	pizza dough shell	1
15 ml	chopped fresh basil	1 tbsp
5 ml	oregano	1 tsp
100 g	grated mozzarella cheese	3½ oz
	salt and pepper	
	few drops of extra virgin olive oil	

Preheat oven to 260°C (500°F, mark 10).

1 Heat oil in frying pan over medium heat. Add onion, garlic and red pepper; season well. Cook 3 minutes.

2 Add sausage meat and continue cooking 4 minutes.

3 Spread pizza sauce over pizza dough shell. Cover with sausage mixture and sprinkle seasonings over meat. Top with cheese.

4 Bake 10 to 12 minutes in oven. Drizzle extra virgin olive oil over pizza just before serving.

Mexican Pizza with Monterey Jack
36-cm (14-in) pizza

60 ml	olive oil	4 tbsp
½	onion, chopped	½
2	spring onions, chopped	2
2	garlic cloves, peeled, crushed and chopped	2
1	tomato, peeled, seeded and diced	1
1 ml	crushed chillies	¼ tsp
175 ml	Spicy Gazpacho Sauce (see p. 39)	6 fl oz
1	pizza dough shell	1
100 g	grated Monterey Jack cheese	3½ oz
75 g	grated Parmesan cheese	2½ oz
	salt and pepper	

Preheat oven to 260°C (500°F, mark 10).

1 Heat half of oil in frying pan over medium heat. Add onions, garlic, tomato and crushed chillies. Season well and cook 6 minutes.

2 Spread gazpacho sauce over pizza dough shell. Top with onion/ tomato mixture and cover with both cheeses. Drizzle remaining olive oil over ingredients and season well.

3 Bake 10 to 12 minutes in oven.

Spicy Tomato and Cheese Pizza
36-cm (14-in) pizza

1	small aubergine	1
60 ml	olive oil	4 tbsp
125 ml	Ratatouille Sauce (see p. 41)	4 fl oz
1	pizza dough shell	1
1	dried chilli pepper, crushed	1
50 ml	Thick Pizza Sauce (see p. 42)	2 fl oz
2	garlic cloves, peeled and sliced	2
135 g	grated mozzarella cheese	4½ oz
	coarse salt	
	freshly ground pepper	
	few drops extra virgin olive oil	

1 Cut aubergine into 10 slices, about 5 mm (¼ in) thick. Spread slices on absorbent kitchen paper and sprinkle with coarse salt. Let stand 30 minutes. Drain and pat dry.

2 Preheat oven to 260 °C (500 °F, mark 10).

3 Heat oil in frying pan over medium heat. Add aubergine slices and cook 3 minutes on each side. Remove and set aside.

4 Spread ratatouille sauce over pizza dough shell. Mix dried chilli pepper with pizza sauce; spread over pizza.

5 Sprinkle garlic over pizza and cover with cheese. Arrange aubergine slices and season well with pepper. Drizzle a few drops of extra virgin olive oil over ingredients.

6 Bake 10 to 12 minutes in oven.

Double Tomato Aubergine Pizza
36-cm (14-in) pizza

60 ml	olive oil	4 tbsp
1	small aubergine, sliced 5 mm (¼ in) thick	1
1	large onion, peeled and chopped small	1
175 ml	Basic Fresh Tomato Sauce (see p. 35)	6 fl oz
1	pizza dough shell	1
12	slices Fontina cheese	12
30 g	sun-dried tomatoes	1 oz
	freshly ground pepper	

Preheat oven to 260°C (500°F, mark 10).

1 Heat 45 ml (3 tbsp) oil in frying pan over high heat. Add aubergine slices and cook 3 minutes on each side. When cooked, remove from pan and set aside.

2 Add remaining oil to hot frying pan. Add onion and reduce heat to medium; cook 6 minutes.

3 Spread tomato sauce over pizza dough shell. Arrange aubergine slices and onion over sauce. Season well with pepper. Cover with slices of cheese and top with sun-dried tomatoes.

4 Bake 10 to 12 minutes in oven.

Pizza Sandwich alla Ricotta
36-cm (14-in) pizza

75 ml	Thick Pizza Sauce (see p. 42)	5 tbsp
I	pizza dough shell	I
225 g	ricotta cheese	½ lb
90 g	mortadella sausage, thinly sliced	3 oz
2	hard-boiled eggs, sliced	2
	few drops olive oil	

Preheat oven to 230°C (450°F, mark 8).

1 Spread pizza sauce over pizza dough shell. It is especially important in this recipe to leave a 1-cm (½-in) border free of sauce.

2 Arrange cheese, sausage and eggs over pizza. Sprinkle with a few drops of oil.

3 Wet edges of dough with cold water. Carefully fold dough in half. Press edges of dough together, forming seal.

4 Bake 20 minutes in oven.

Ham and Sausage Pizza with Chutney
36-cm (14-in) pizza

30 ml	olive oil	2 tbsp
100 g	cooked ham, cut in strips	3½ oz
100 g	mortadella sausage, cut in strips	3½ oz
90 ml	chutney	6 tbsp
250 ml	Ratatouille Sauce (see p. 41)	8 fl oz
1	pizza dough shell	1
10	slices Scamorze cheese	10
75 g	stoned Kalamata olives, chopped	2½ oz
	freshly ground pepper	
	few drops of extra virgin olive oil	

Preheat oven to 260 °C (500 °F, mark 10).

1 Heat olive oil in frying pan over medium heat. Add ham and sausage; cook 2 minutes. Stir in chutney and continue cooking 1 minute. Set aside.

2 Spread ratatouille sauce over pizza dough shell. Add ham and sausage mixture and cover with slices of cheese. Season with pepper.

3 Top with chopped olives and drizzle a few drops of extra virgin olive oil over ingredients.

4 Bake 10 to 12 minutes in oven.

Asparagus Pizza with Scamorze
36-cm (14-in) pizza

2	bunches fresh asparagus	2
30 g	butter	1 oz
1	sweet yellow pepper, chopped	1
250 ml	White Sauce, heated (see p. 38)	8 fl oz
1	pizza dough shell	1
90 g	grated Scamorze cheese	3 oz
75 g	stoned black olives, sliced	2½ oz
90 g	grated Gruyère cheese	3 oz
	salt and black pepper	
	cayenne pepper to taste	

Preheat oven to 260°C (500°F, mark 10).

1 Pare asparagus if necessary and trim stem ends. Soak briefly in cold water, then cut stalks into 2.5-cm (1-in) pieces. Steam just until tender.

2 Heat butter in frying pan over medium heat. Add asparagus and chopped yellow pepper. Cook 3 minutes.

3 Spread white sauce over pizza dough shell. Add Scamorze cheese and top with hot vegetables; season well. Add olives and cover with Gruyère cheese. Season with black pepper and cayenne pepper to taste.

4 Bake 10 to 12 minutes in oven.

Hawaiian Pizza
36-cm (14-in) pizza

175 ml	Basic Fresh Tomato Sauce (see p. 35)	6 fl oz
1	pizza dough shell	1
150 g	sliced cooked mushrooms	5 oz
275 g	cooked diced lobster meat	10 oz
135 g	grated mozzarella cheese	4½ oz
150 g	diced pineapple	5 oz
	salt and pepper	
	paprika to taste	

Preheat oven to 260°C (500°F, mark 10).

1 Spread tomato sauce over pizza dough shell. Top with mushrooms and lobster meat and cover with cheese. Season with salt and pepper.

2 Top with diced pineapple. Season with paprika to taste.

3 Bake 10 to 12 minutes in oven.

Cheese Lover's Pizza
36-cm (14-in) pizza

125 ml	Pesto Sauce (see p. 37)	4 fl oz
1	pizza dough shell	1
2	large tomatoes, cored	2
2	garlic cloves, peeled and thinly sliced	2
225 g	Bel Paese cheese, diced	1/2 lb
	freshly ground pepper	
	extra virgin olive oil	

Preheat oven to 260°C (500°F, mark 10).

1 Spread pesto sauce over pizza dough shell. Slice tomatoes about 5 mm (¼ in) thick and arrange on pizza.

2 Scatter sliced garlic over pizza and season with pepper. Top with diced cheese and drizzle with a few drops of extra virgin olive oil.

3 Bake 10 to 12 minutes in oven.

Pizza à la Rouille
36-cm (14-in) pizza

1½	sweet green peppers	1½
1	pizza dough shell	1
125 ml	Rouille Pizza Spread (see p. 40)	4 fl oz
90 g	grated Pecorino cheese	3 oz
175 ml	Fresh Tomato Sauté (see p. 36)	6 fl oz
15 ml	olive oil	1 tbsp
	freshly ground pepper	

Preheat oven to 260°C (500°F, mark 10).

1 Cut green peppers in half and remove seeds. Oil skin and place cut-side-down on baking sheet; grill 6 minutes. Remove and let cool. Peel off skin, slice and set aside.

2 Cover pizza dough shell with thin layer of rouille pizza spread.

3 Arrange cheese, sliced green peppers and fresh tomato sauté over sauce.

4 Drizzle olive oil over ingredients and season with pepper.

5 Bake 10 to 12 minutes in oven.

Tasty Clam Pizza
36-cm (14-in) pizza

15 ml	olive oil	1 tbsp
1	pizza dough shell	1
2	garlic cloves, peeled and thinly sliced	2
175 ml	Basic Fresh Tomato Sauce (see p. 35)	6 fl oz
10	slices Provolone cheese	10
175 g	canned clams, drained	6 oz
45 ml	grated Parmesan cheese	3 tbsp
	freshly ground pepper	

Preheat oven to 260 °C (500 °F, mark 10).

1 Brush oil over pizza dough shell and add garlic. Spread tomato sauce over pizza and top with Provolone cheese. Season well with pepper.

2 Bake 10 to 12 minutes in oven.

3 About 4 minutes before pizza is done, add clams and Parmesan cheese. Complete baking.

Pizza with Fresh Oyster Mushrooms
36-cm (14-in) pizza

45 ml	olive oil	3 tbsp
1	large red onion, peeled and cut in rings	1
4	large tomatoes, peeled, seeded and roughly chopped	4
30 g	butter	1 oz
8	fresh oyster mushrooms, thickly sliced	8
1	pizza dough shell	1
100 g	grated Monterey Jack cheese	3 1/2 oz
75 g	diced leftover cooked chicken	2 1/2 oz
	salt and pepper	

Preheat oven to 260°C (500°F, mark 10).

1 Heat oil in frying pan over medium heat. Add onion and cook 8 minutes. Add tomatoes, season and continue cooking 15 minutes.

2 Heat butter in small frying pan over medium heat. Add oyster mushrooms and sauté 2 to 3 minutes.

3 Spread tomato mixture over pizza dough shell. Add mushrooms and top with grated cheese. Season with pepper.

4 Bake 10 to 12 minutes in oven.

5 About 4 minutes before pizza is done, add chopped chicken and complete baking.

Onion Pizza with Gorgonzola Cheese
36-cm (14-in) pizza
(or 4 individual-sized pizzas)

60 ml	olive oil	4 tbsp
2	large onions, peeled and thinly sliced	2
1	pizza dough shell	1
75 g	pine nuts	2½ oz
350 g	crumbled Gorgonzola cheese	¾ lb
12	fresh basil leaves	12
	salt and freshly ground pepper	

Preheat oven to 260°C (500°F, mark 10).

1 Heat 45 ml (3 tbsp) oil in frying pan over medium heat. Add onions, season and cook 15 minutes. Reduce heat if onions brown too quickly.

2 Cover bottom of pizza dough shell with cooked onions. Add pine nuts and top with cheese. Arrange basil leaves and drizzle remaining oil over ingredients. Season with pepper.

3 Bake 10 to 12 minutes in oven.

Fennel and Leek Pizza
36-cm (14-in) pizza

2	small leeks, white part only	2
1	small fennel bulb	1
45 ml	olive oil	3 tbsp
1	shallot, peeled and chopped	1
1	pizza dough shell	1
125 ml	Rouille Pizza Spread (see p. 40)	4 fl oz
135 g	grated Fontina cheese	4 1/2 oz
60 g	stoned green olives, sliced	2 oz
30 g	grated Parmesan cheese	1 oz
	salt and pepper	

Preheat oven to 260°C (500°F, mark 10).

1 Slit leeks from top to bottom twice, leaving 2.5 cm (1 in) intact at base. Wash leeks under cold, running water to remove grit and sand. Drain and slice thinly.

2 Peel fennel and slice thinly. Heat oil in frying pan over medium heat. Add fennel, leeks and shallot. Season, cover and cook 18 minutes over low heat. Stir occasionally to prevent sticking.

3 Cover pizza dough shell with rouille spread. Add cooked fennel and leeks.

4 Cover pizza with Fontina cheese. Top with olives and Parmesan cheese. Season well with pepper.

5 Bake 10 to 12 minutes in oven.

Pizza with Sautéed Chicken and Fontina
36-cm (14-in) pizza

45 ml	olive oil	3 tbsp
1	whole skinned boneless chicken breast, thinly sliced	1
2	shallots, peeled and chopped	2
2	spring onions, chopped	2
15 ml	chopped fresh basil	1 tbsp
5 ml	herbes de Provence	1 tsp
30 g	pine nuts	1 oz
175 ml	Thick Pizza Sauce (see p. 42)	6 fl oz
1	pizza dough shell	1
100 g	diced Fontina cheese	3½ oz
	salt and pepper	

Preheat oven to 260°C (500°F, mark 10).

1 Heat oil in frying pan over medium heat. Add chicken strips, season and cook 2 minutes on each side. Add shallots, spring onions, seasonings and pine nuts. Continue cooking 1 minute, then set aside.

2 Spread pizza sauce over pizza dough shell. Add chicken mixture and top with cheese. Season well with pepper.

3 Bake 10 to 12 minutes in oven.

Pizza with Cooked Garlic and Japanese Aubergine
36-cm (14-in) pizza

60 ml	olive oil	4 tbsp
1	garlic bulb, separated into cloves	1
1	Japanese («baby») aubergine	1
175 ml	Thick Pizza Sauce (see p. 42)	6 fl oz
1	pizza dough shell	1
160 g	grated Fontina cheese	5½ oz
45 ml	chopped fresh basil	3 tbsp
	freshly ground pepper	
	few drops extra virgin olive oil	

Preheat oven to 200 °C (400 °F, mark 6).

1 Heat 45 ml (3 tbsp) oil in frying pan over medium heat. Add garlic cloves (do not peel) and cook 15 minutes. Reduce heat if necessary to prevent burning. Remove, let cool and peel cloves.

2 Meanwhile, cut aubergine into slices about 5 mm (¼ in) thick. Brush both sides with 15 ml (1 tbsp) oil. Bake 12 minutes in oven, turning slices over once.

3 Increase oven temperature to 260 °C (500 °F, mark 10).

4 Spread pizza sauce over pizza dough shell. Cover with cheese and top with aubergine slices and garlic cloves.

5 Season with pepper. Sprinkle with basil and a few drops of extra virgin olive oil.

6 Bake 10 to 12 minutes in oven.

Artichoke and Aubergine Sauce Pizza
36-cm (14-in) pizza

45 ml	olive oil	3 tbsp
3	onions, peeled and thinly sliced	3
250 ml	Ratatouille Sauce (see p. 41)	8 fl oz
1	pizza dough shell	1
8	artichoke hearts, marinated in oil, drained and quartered	8
15 ml	chopped fresh basil	1 tbsp
45 ml	grated Parmesan cheese	3 tbsp
160 g	grated Fontina cheese	5½ oz
	freshly ground pepper	

Preheat oven to 260°C (500°F, mark 10).

1 Heat oil in frying pan over medium heat. Add onions and cook 15 minutes over low heat. Do not let onions burn.

2 Spread ratatouille sauce over pizza dough shell. Add onions, artichoke hearts and basil.

3 Top with grated cheeses and season well with pepper.

4 Bake 10 to 12 minutes in oven.

Cajun Chicken Pizza
36-cm (14-in) pizza

45 g	butter	1 ½ oz
½	small onion, chopped	½
½	celery stick, diced	½
1	sweet red or green pepper, sliced	1
1	whole skinned boneless chicken breast	1
2 ml	oregano	½ tsp
175 ml	Basic Fresh Tomato Sauce (see p. 35)	6 fl oz
1	pizza dough shell	1
15 ml	chopped fresh basil	1 tbsp
135 g	grated smoked mozzarella cheese	4 ½ oz
	pinch of cayenne pepper	
	pinch of thyme	
	salt and white pepper	

Preheat oven to 260°C (500°F, mark 10).

1 Heat butter in frying pan over medium heat. Add onion, celery and red pepper; cook 2 minutes.

2 Split chicken breast into two. Add to vegetables in pan and cook 2 minutes on each side. Add oregano, cayenne pepper, thyme, salt and white pepper. Mix well and cover pan. Cook chicken 10 to 12 minutes over low heat. Set pan aside.

3 Spread tomato sauce over pizza dough shell. Add chopped basil and grated cheese. Place pizza in oven and bake 8 minutes.

4 Remove pizza from oven. Slice chicken breasts and arrange on pizza. Top with chopped vegetables and continue baking for 3 to 4 minutes.

Greek Pizza Pie
36-cm (14-in) pizza

I	medium aubergine	I
60 ml	olive oil	4 tbsp
I	pizza dough shell	I
250 ml	Fresh Tomato Sauté (see p. 36)	8 fl oz
75 g	feta cheese, crumbled	2½ oz
30 g	stoned black olives, sliced	I oz
	freshly ground pepper	

Preheat oven to 260°C (500°F, mark 10).

1 Cut aubergine into 12 round slices. Heat 45 ml (3 tbsp) oil in frying pan over medium heat. Cook aubergine slices 2 minutes on each side over high heat; set aside.

2 Brush dough with remaining olive oil. Spread sautéed tomatoes over dough and add cheese.

3 Arrange aubergine slices on pizza and top with sliced olives. Season with pepper.

4 Bake 10 to 12 minutes in oven.

Red Salsa Pizza with Pepperoni
36-cm (14-in) pizza

1	large sweet red pepper	1
2	sweet green peppers	2
250 ml	wine vinegar	8 fl oz
45 ml	sugar	3 tbsp
2	tomatoes, peeled, seeded and chopped	2
2	spring onions, chopped	2
2	garlic cloves, peeled, crushed and chopped	2
1	jalapeño pepper, seeded and chopped	1
1	pizza dough shell	1
135 g	grated mozzarella cheese	4 1/2 oz
15	slices pepperoni	15
75 g	stoned black olives, chopped	2 1/2 oz
	salt and pepper	
	few drops extra virgin olive oil	

Preheat oven to 260°C (500°F, mark 10).

1 Cut red and green peppers in half and remove seeds. Oil skin and place cut-side-down on baking sheet; grill 8 minutes. Remove and place in large bowl. Cover bowl with cling film. Let peppers steam 3 minutes. Peel and discard skins. Dice peppers and place in mixing bowl; set aside.

2 Place vinegar and sugar in small saucepan. Cook until liquid becomes golden in colour. Pour over diced peppers in mixing bowl.

3 Add tomatoes, spring onions, garlic and jalapeño pepper; mix and season well. Marinate 5 minutes.

4 Spread salsa over pizza dough shell. Add cheese and pepperoni. Top with chopped olives. Sprinkle with a few drops of extra virgin olive oil.

5 Bake 10 to 12 minutes in oven.

Garden Fresh Pizza
36-cm (14-in) pizza

1	small bunch fresh asparagus	1
1	small head broccoli	1
45 ml	olive oil	3 tbsp
1	large carrot, pared and thinly sliced	1
2	garlic cloves, peeled, crushed and chopped	2
250 ml	White Sauce, heated (see p. 38)	8 fl oz
1	pizza dough shell	1
160 g	grated Gruyère cheese	5½ oz
	salt and pepper	
	pinch of paprika	
	few drops of extra virgin olive oil	

Preheat oven to 260 °C (500 °F, mark 10).

1 Pare asparagus if necessary and trim stem ends. Soak briefly in cold water, then cut stalks into 2.5-cm (1-in) pieces. Divide broccoli into small florets.

2 Heat oil in frying pan over medium heat. Add asparagus, broccoli, carrot and garlic. Season, cover and cook 6 to 8 minutes over low heat.

3 Spread white sauce over pizza dough shell. Add cooked vegetables and top with cheese. Season well and sprinkle with paprika. Drizzle a few drops of extra virgin olive oil over ingredients.

4 Bake 10 to 12 minutes in oven.

Black Olive Pizza with Pecorino Cheese
36-cm (14-in) pizza

45 ml	olive oil	3 tbsp
1	onion, peeled and finely chopped	1
175 ml	Basic Fresh Tomato Sauce (see p. 35)	6 fl oz
1	pizza dough shell	1
2	garlic cloves, peeled and thinly sliced	2
60 g	grated Pecorino cheese	2 oz
45 g	stoned black olives, sliced	1 ½ oz
	freshly ground pepper	

Preheat oven to 260 °C (500 °F, mark 10).

1 Heat half of oil in frying pan over medium heat. Add chopped onion and cook 5 minutes over low heat.

2 Spread tomato sauce over pizza dough shell. Sprinkle cooked onion and garlic over sauce.

3 Add cheese, then black olives. Drizzle remaining oil over ingredients and season with pepper.

4 Bake 10 to 12 minutes in oven.

Artichoke Pizza
36-cm (14-in) pizza

45 g	butter	1½ oz
1	shallot, peeled and chopped	1
10	fresh mushrooms, cleaned and sliced	10
175 ml	Thick Pizza Sauce (see p. 42)	6 fl oz
1	pizza dough shell	1
75 g	grated mozzarella cheese	2½ oz
60 g	prosciutto, sliced	2 oz
8	artichoke hearts, marinated in oil	8
30 g	stoned black olives, sliced	1 oz
15 ml	olive oil	1 tbsp
15 ml	chopped fresh basil	1 tbsp
	salt and freshly ground pepper	

Preheat oven to 260 °C (500 °F, mark 10).

1 Heat butter in frying pan over medium heat. Add shallot and mushrooms; season well. Cook 4 minutes.

2 Spread pizza sauce over pizza dough shell. Arrange cooked mushrooms over sauce. Add cheese and prosciutto.

3 Drain artichoke hearts, slice in half and place on pizza with black olives. Drizzle oil over ingredients and sprinkle with basil.

4 Bake 10 to 12 minutes in oven.

Pizza Provençale
two 36-cm (14-in) pizzas

125 ml	olive oil	4 fl oz
4	onions, peeled and finely chopped	4
3	garlic cloves, peeled	3
3	sprigs fresh parsley	3
2 ml	thyme	½ tsp
2	pizza dough shells	2
18	anchovy fillets	18
24	stoned black olives, halved	24
	freshly ground pepper	
	grated Parmesan cheese to taste	

Preheat oven to 260°C (500°F, mark 10).

1 Heat oil in frying pan over medium heat. Add onions, whole garlic cloves, parsley and thyme. Season with pepper and cook 20 minutes over medium heat. Onions should become golden in colour, but not brown.

2 When cooked, discard garlic and parsley sprigs. Spread onions over pizza dough shells.

3 Drain anchovy fillets and rinse under cold water. Drain again and pat dry with absorbent kitchen paper. Arrange fillets on pizzas.

4 Top with black olives and grated Parmesan cheese to taste.

5 Bake 10 to 12 minutes in oven.

Pesto Pizza with Sun-Dried Tomatoes

36-cm (14-in) pizza
(or 4 individual-sized pizzas)

30 ml	cornmeal	2 tbsp
1	pizza dough shell	1
125 ml	Pesto Sauce (see p. 37)	4 fl oz
135 g	grated mozzarella cheese	4 1/2 oz
15 g	chopped sun-dried tomatoes	1/2 oz
30 g	pine nuts	1 oz
	freshly ground pepper	
	few drops of olive oil	

Preheat oven to 260 °C (500 °F, mark 10).

1 Line oiled pizza pan with cornmeal and position pizza dough shell.

2 Spread pesto sauce over pizza. Add cheese, sun-dried tomatoes and pine nuts. Season well with pepper. Drizzle a few drops of oil over ingredients.

3 Bake 10 to 12 minutes in oven.

Party Pizza Muffins
(8 servings)

200 g	grated Pecorino Sardo cheese	7 oz
100 g	grated mature cheddar cheese	3½ oz
375 ml	Thick Pizza Sauce (see p. 42)	12 fl oz
30 ml	chopped fresh basil	2 tbsp
3	garlic cloves, peeled, crushed and chopped	3
1	jalapeño pepper, seeded and chopped	1
8	English muffins, split in half	8
	salt and pepper	

Preheat oven to 230°C (450°F, mark 8).

1 Place all ingredients, except muffins, in food processor. Blend several seconds until combined.

2 Arrange split English muffins on baking sheets. Top each with pizza mixture and bake 10 to 12 minutes in oven.

Tasty Sausage Pizza
36-cm (14-in) pizza

45 ml	olive oil	3 tbsp
150 g	Italian sausage, sliced	1/3 lb
1/2	sweet green pepper, thinly sliced	1/2
60 g	sliced pimiento pepper	2 oz
1	onion, peeled and thinly sliced	1
1 ml	crushed chillies	1/4 tsp
1	pizza dough shell	1
175 ml	Thick Pizza Sauce (see p. 42)	6 fl oz
135 g	grated mozzarella cheese	4 1/2 oz
30 g	grated Romano cheese	1 oz
	salt and black pepper	

Preheat oven to 260°C (500°F, mark 10).

1 Heat 30 ml (2 tbsp) oil in frying pan over medium heat. Add sausage, green pepper, pimiento, onion, and crushed chillies. Season well and cook 4 minutes.

2 Spread sausage mixture over pizza dough shell. Cover with pizza sauce and top with mozzarella and Romano cheeses. Season well with black pepper and drizzle remaining oil over ingredients.

3 Bake 10 to 12 minutes in oven.

Cocktail Party Pizza
36-cm (14-in) pizza

2	apples	2
175 g	Brie cheese, chilled	6 oz
1	pizza dough shell	1
60 g	blue cheese, crumbled	2 oz
	few drops of lemon juice	
	few drops of olive oil	
	freshly ground pepper	

Preheat oven to 260 °C (500 °F, mark 10).

1 Core, peel and slice apples. Place in bowl and toss with lemon juice to prevent discolouring.

2 Remove rind from Brie cheese and discard. Cut cheese into small pieces.

3 Arrange sliced apples in a circle pattern on pizza dough shell. Top with pieces of Brie and crumbled blue cheese.

4 Drizzle olive oil over cheeses and season well with pepper.

5 Bake a maximum of 10 minutes in oven.

Sliced Tomato Pizza with Provolone
36-cm (14-in) pizza

30 ml	olive oil	2 tbsp
1	pizza dough shell	1
2	tomatoes, cored, peeled and thickly sliced	2
2	garlic cloves, peeled and thinly sliced	2
30 ml	chopped fresh basil	2 tbsp
5 ml	oregano	1 tsp
60 g	grated Provolone cheese	2 oz
90 g	grated mozzarella cheese	3 oz
4	rashers crisp cooked bacon, chopped	4
	salt and freshly ground pepper	

Preheat oven to 260°C (500°F, mark 10).

1 Brush olive oil over pizza dough shell.

2 Arrange tomato slices on pizza. Add garlic, basil and oregano. Season well.

3 Add grated Provolone cheese and pepper. Add mozzarella cheese.

4 Bake 10 to 12 minutes in oven.

5 About 3 minutes before pizza is done, add chopped bacon and complete baking.

Bocconcini Pizza

36-cm (14-in) pizza

250 ml	Thick Pizza Sauce (see p. 42)	8 fl oz
1	pizza dough shell	1
90 g	diced Bocconcini cheese	3 oz
15 g	fresh basil leaves	1/2 oz
2 ml	oregano	1/2 tsp
45 ml	olive oil	3 tbsp
	freshly ground pepper	

Preheat oven to 260 °C (500 °F, mark 10).

1 Spread pizza sauce over pizza dough shell.

2 Arrange cheese, basil leaves and oregano over pizza. Drizzle olive oil over ingredients and season generously with pepper.

3 Bake 10 to 12 minutes in oven.

Ratatouille Pizza with Pepperoni and Mushrooms
36-cm (14-in) pizza

I	small chilli pepper, seeded and chopped	I
250 ml	Ratatouille Sauce (see p. 41)	8 fl oz
I	pizza dough shell	I
90 g	grated mozzarella cheese	3 oz
15	slices pepperoni	15
6	fresh mushrooms, cleaned and sliced	6
6	fresh basil leaves	6
30 ml	olive oil	2 tbsp
	freshly ground pepper	

Preheat oven to 260°C (500°F, mark 10).

1 Mix chopped chilli pepper with ratatouille sauce. Spread over pizza dough shell.

2 Add cheese, pepperoni, mushrooms and basil leaves. Drizzle oil over ingredients and season with pepper.

3 Bake 10 to 12 minutes in oven.

Shallot Pizza with Kalamata Olives
36-cm (14-in) pizza

60 ml	olive oil	4 tbsp
900 g	shallots, peeled	2 lb
15 ml	brown sugar	1 tbsp
225 g	fresh mushrooms, cleaned and sliced	½ lb
1	pizza dough shell	1
125 g	prosciutto, sliced 1 cm (½ in) wide	¼ lb
1	garlic clove, peeled and sliced	1
135 g	grated Fontina cheese	4½ oz
75 g	stoned Kalamata olives, halved	2½ oz
4	anchovy fillets, drained and chopped	4
	salt and pepper	
	extra virgin olive oil	

1 Heat 45 ml (3 tbsp) oil in frying pan over medium heat. Add shallots and season; cook 30 minutes over low heat.

2 Add brown sugar, mix and cook 3 minutes. Remove shallots from pan and set aside.

3 Preheat oven to 260°C (500°F, mark 10).

4 Add remaining oil to hot pan. Cook mushrooms 3 minutes over high heat.

5 Arrange shallots over pizza dough shell. Add mushrooms and season with pepper. Add prosciutto and garlic. Cover with cheese.

6 Top with olives and anchovies. Sprinkle with extra virgin olive oil.

7 Bake 10 to 12 minutes in oven.

Prawn Pizza with Purée of Sweet Peppers
36-cm (14-in) pizza

3	sweet red peppers	3
2	sweet green peppers	2
1	sweet yellow pepper	1
6	garlic cloves, unpeeled	6
50 ml	Thick Pizza Sauce (see p. 42)	2 fl oz
1	pizza dough shell	1
135 g	grated Fontina cheese	4½ oz
225 g	fresh prawns, peeled and deveined	½ lb
75 g	stoned black olives, sliced	2½ oz
15 ml	chopped fresh basil	1 tbsp
	freshly ground black pepper	
	few drops of olive oil	

Preheat oven to 260 °C (500 °F, mark 10).

1 Cut peppers in half and remove seeds. Oil skin and place cut-side-down on baking sheet; grill 15 to 18 minutes. Turn peppers over once during cooking. Remove and place in large bowl. Cover bowl with cling film. Let peppers steam 3 minutes. Peel and discard skins.

2 Place unpeeled garlic cloves in saucepan with 250 ml (8 fl oz) water. Bring to boil and cook 4 minutes. Remove cloves from water and let cool. Peel and purée flesh.

3 Place peppers in food processor with garlic. Blend together for several seconds. Add pizza sauce, season and blend well.

4 Spread pepper mixture over pizza dough shell. Top with cheese and bake 6 minutes in oven.

5 Slice prawns in half and arrange on pizza. Add olives and basil; season well with black pepper. Continue baking for 4 to 6 minutes.

6 Sprinkle with a few drops of olive oil before serving.

Pizza à la Crème
36-cm (14-in) pizza

45 ml	olive oil	3 tbsp
350 g	fresh mushrooms, cleaned and sliced	¾ lb
2	shallots, peeled and chopped	2
250 ml	White Sauce, heated (see p. 38)	8 fl oz
1	pizza dough shell	1
135 g	grated mozzarella cheese	4½ oz
3	rashers crisp cooked bacon, chopped	3
	salt and pepper	
	paprika to taste	

Preheat oven to 260 °C (500 °F, mark 10).

1 Heat oil in frying pan over medium heat. Add mushrooms and shallots. Season and cook 5 minutes over high heat. Remove and set aside.

2 Spread white sauce over pizza dough shell. Cover with mushrooms and top with cheese. Season generously with pepper and paprika to taste.

3 Bake 10 to 12 minutes in oven.

4 About 2 minutes before pizza is done, add chopped bacon and complete baking.

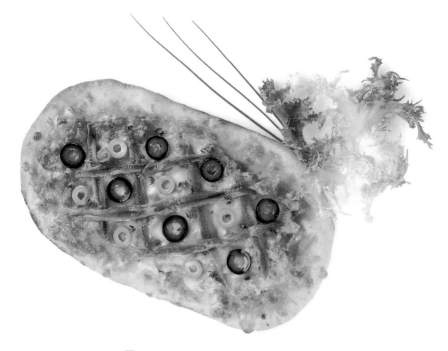

Double Olive Tomato Pizza
36-cm (14-in) pizza

15	anchovy fillets, drained	15
45 ml	milk	3 tbsp
30 ml	olive oil	2 tbsp
3	tomatoes, peeled, seeded and chopped	3
2	garlic cloves, peeled, crushed and chopped	2
15 ml	chopped fresh basil	1 tbsp
1 ml	thyme	1/4 tsp
1 ml	oregano	1/4 tsp
1	pizza dough shell	1
160 g	grated mozzarella cheese	5 1/2 oz
30 g	stoned green olives, sliced	1 oz
30 g	stoned black olives, sliced	1 oz
	freshly ground pepper	

Preheat oven to 260 °C (500 °F, mark 10).

1 Soak anchovy fillets in milk for 3 minutes. Remove and set aside to drain on absorbent kitchen paper.

2 Heat oil in frying pan over medium heat. Add tomatoes, garlic and seasonings. Cook 8 minutes.

3 Spread hot tomato mixture over pizza dough shell. Cover with cheese and add green olives.

4 Arrange anchovy fillets in lattice pattern and decorate with black olives. Season with pepper.

5 Bake 10 to 12 minutes in oven.

Leek and Ham Pizza
36-cm (14-in) pizza

4	leeks, white part only	4
45 ml	olive oil	3 tbsp
15 ml	mixed herbs (parsley,oregano,marjoram)	1 tbsp
1	pizza dough shell	1
90 g	cooked ham, cut in julienne	3 oz
60 g	prosciutto, sliced 1 cm (½ in) wide	2 oz
45 ml	grated Parmesan cheese	3 tbsp
60 g	diced mozzarella cheese	2 oz
	juice of ½ lemon	
	salt and pepper	

Preheat oven to 260°C (500°F, mark 10).

1 Slit leeks from top to bottom twice, leaving 2.5 cm (1 in) intact at base. Wash leeks under cold, running water to remove grit and sand.

2 Place leeks in boiling, salted water. Add lemon juice and cook 15 minutes over medium heat.

3 Remove leeks from water and set aside to drain. When cool enough to handle, squeeze out excess liquid, then slice.

4 Heat 30 ml (2 tbsp) oil in frying pan over medium heat. Add leeks and mixed herbs; cook 3 minutes.

5 Spread leeks over pizza dough shell. Add ham and prosciutto; top with cheeses. Season well with pepper and drizzle remaining oil over ingredients.

6 Bake 10 to 12 minutes in oven.

Fyllo Pizza
(6 to 8 servings)

150 g	melted butter	5 oz
14	sheets fyllo dough, 30 x 40 cm (12 x 16 in)	14
75 g	grated Parmesan cheese	2½ oz
45 ml	olive oil	3 tbsp
2	onions, peeled and thinly sliced	2
2	garlic cloves, peeled, crushed and chopped	2
30 ml	chopped fresh basil	2 tbsp
135 g	grated mozzarella cheese	4½ oz
4	large tomatoes, cored and sliced 5 mm (¼ in) thick	4
	salt and pepper	

Preheat oven to 190°C (375°F, mark 5).

1 Brush large ovenproof baking dish* with melted butter. Position first sheet of fyllo dough in bottom and sprinkle with Parmesan cheese. Add next sheet of dough, brush with melted butter and sprinkle with Parmesan. Repeat for remaining sheets of dough.

2 Heat 30 ml (2 tbsp) oil in frying pan over medium heat. Add onions, garlic and basil. Season well and cook 4 minutes. Spoon mixture over top layer of dough.

3 Cover with mozzarella cheese. Top with tomato slices and sprinkle with remaining Parmesan cheese. Drizzle remaining olive oil over tomatoes. Season with pepper.

4 Bake 30 to 40 minutes in oven.

*Dish should be large enough to accommodate fyllo sheets, and about 5 cm (2 in) deep.

Fresh Mushroom and Red Pepper Pizza
36-cm (14-in) pizza

1	pizza dough shell	1
150 ml	Fresh Tomato Sauté (see p. 36)	5 fl oz
100 g	grated Provolone cheese	3¹/₂ oz
25 g	grated Parmesan cheese	1 oz
16	large fresh mushrooms, cleaned and sliced	16
1	sweet red pepper, sliced	1
	extra virgin olive oil	
	salt and pepper	

Preheat oven to 260°C (500°F, mark 10).

1 Drizzle small amount of olive oil over pizza dough shell. Spread fresh tomato sauté over dough and top with cheeses.

2 Arrange mushrooms and red pepper over cheeses. Season well with salt and pepper.

3 Bake 10 to 12 minutes in oven.

Goat Cheese and Bacon Pizza
36-cm (14-in) pizza

350 g	goat cheese	¾ lb
50 ml	soured cream	2 fl oz
45 g	chopped pimiento pepper	1½ oz
1	pizza dough shell	1
175 ml	Thick Pizza Sauce (see p. 42)	6 fl oz
75 g	grated Parmesan cheese	2½ oz
5	rashers crisp cooked bacon, chopped	5
	few drops of Tabasco sauce	
	few drops of Worcestershire sauce	
	salt and pepper	

Preheat oven to 260°C (500°F, mark 10).

1 Place goat cheese, soured cream, pimiento pepper, and Tabasco and Worcestershire sauces in food processor. Season well and blend thoroughly.

2 Spread cheese mixture over pizza dough shell. Cover with pizza sauce and Parmesan cheese. Season with pepper.

3 Bake 10 to 12 minutes in oven.

4 About 3 minutes before pizza is done, add chopped bacon and complete baking.

Pizza Romana
36-cm (14-in) pizza

250 ml	Thick Pizza Sauce (see p. 42)	8 fl oz
1	pizza dough shell	1
100 g	diced mozzarella cheese	3 ½ oz
1 ml	oregano	¼ tsp
15 ml	chopped fresh basil	1 tbsp
8	anchovy fillets, drained	8
	few drops of olive oil	
	freshly ground pepper	

Preheat oven to 260°C (500°F, mark 10).

1 Spread pizza sauce over pizza dough shell.

2 Add cheese and seasonings. Arrange anchovy fillets on pizza to resemble spokes of a wheel. Drizzle a few drops of olive oil over pizza and season with pepper.

3 Bake 10 to 12 minutes in oven.

Index